MW00417194

101 PRODUCT IDEAS FOR AMAZON FBA

What to Sell on Amazon in 2020

Matt Voss

DISTRICT HOUSE

Inc., is implied. Wherever the words "Amazon" or "FBA" appear in this book, they are used in an editorial context to refer to the company Amazon and its service, FBA.

CONTENTS

Read This First

As a thank-you for buying this book, I'd like to offer you the free *Amazon FBA Master Spreadsheet*.

This is the exact same spreadsheet I've used for years to find winning products on Amazon. I **highly** recommend you use the Master Spreadsheet as a supplement to your product research. It's the best way to organize and maintain all of the product research and analysis you will perform as an Amazon seller.

Also, be sure to pick up my guide for beginners, *7 FBA Secrets That Turn Beginners into Best Sellers*, which takes you through exactly how to use the spreadsheet to assess market competition and find winning products.

If you're serious about learning how to make an income selling on Amazon, go to the link above and get the Master Spreadsheet today.

In it, you will find: *a)* Step-by-step instructions on how to sell on Amazon FBA, *b)* A tool for conducting product research and analyzing competition on Amazon, *c)* A place to organize and maintain all of your supplier information, keywords, and product copy, and *d)* Bonus tips not included in the book.

Get the free Master Spreadsheet now! (See last page for links.)

Introduction

The hardest part of getting started on Amazon is finding the right products to sell. Product research is not easy, and if your first product is not successful, you stand to lose not only **thousands of dollars**, but potentially any chance of starting a successful business.

The first product you sell on Amazon is likely going to make or break your business

That is the reality. Unless you have endless amounts of money to invest (in which case you probably don't need to be selling on Amazon), the first product you choose to sell will likely determine the success of your business. The profits you make on your first product will afford you the ability to invest in more products and expand your business. And so naturally, selecting your first product can seem like a daunting task.

Are you thinking about selling on Amazon or are in the process of finding your first product? Do you feel you've learned more or less everything you need to learn to start selling, but are *still* struggling to pull the trigger on a product?

If so, you've come to the right place, because in this book, I'm going to do something *no Amazon seller has ever done before*:

I am going to give you my personal list of the best products to sell on Amazon.

Now why on earth would I do this? Shouldn't I keep this list private and sell the products myself?

I have two things to say about this.

First, my goal in writing this book is to enable new sellers to become successful on Amazon. I've seen too many people lose money on failed business ventures and give up on their dreams of attaining financial freedom. My hope is for this book to help kick-start fledgling Amazon businesses and enable people to *lead better lives*—this is my why. This is why I do what I do. I want to do *whatever* I can to help you succeed, and this includes giving you my list of the best products to sell on Amazon.

Second, the fact that I'm providing this list should indicate to you my confidence in Amazon as one of the best (if not *the* best) ways to make an income online. Many people believe that Amazon has gotten too competitive, but this is simply **not true** (in my guide for beginners, I explain why). This is *only* a list of 101 products to sell on Amazon— in reality, there are many more. I am confident that I will continue to find products beyond this list to sell in the future, and in time you will be too.

In the proceeding pages you will find what are in my judgement the 101 best products to sell on Amazon in 2020. I've grouped them according to their respective product categories (Health and Household, Office Products, etc.), and they are presented in no particular order. For each product I'll explain why it's a potentially profitable product to sell, and finally give it a score: ★★★★★ (5 stars, Amazing product), ★★★★ (4 stars, Great product), or ★★★ (3 stars, Good product).

As we go through the list, my hope is that you begin to form an understanding of the types of products that do well on Amazon. As the marketplace grows increasingly competitive, the types of products that do well are becoming increasingly **obscure**.

Some of the products on this list you may have never heard of or would never think to sell. These are the types of products you should be looking to sell on Amazon.

Finally, in this book you'll find several concepts, such as determining a *unique competitive advantage* and assessing *market competition*, that I assume you already know. All of these concepts and more are covered in full detail in my guide for beginners. In order for you to get the most value out of this book, I *highly* recommend you read the guide either before or while you go through this list. Without the guide you will not be able to fully grasp the logic and content in this book.

Let's begin.

Arts, Crafts, and Sewing

☆Product Idea #1☆
Earring Backs

Score: ☆☆☆☆

In my guide for beginners, I mention the "sweet spot" for the price of a product to be $15-40. While earring backs generally fall below this range, they still make for an attractive product to sell, as the number of sales for earring backs are estimated to be very high. High sales means that you can generally operate with a lower profit margin—in other words, *operating on high volume.*

Searching for "earring backs" on Amazon yields over 6,000 results, which is on the higher side; however, there are plenty of listings on the front page with a very low number of reviews, which indicates that it wouldn't be too difficult to get on the first page.

Furthermore, earring backs have a favorable level of *differentiation*, meaning there are several ways to differentiate this product and make it stand out, such as (to name a few) the design of the earring backs themselves, the box that they come in, and the material they are made of.

Finally, the product is very light, leading to lower shipping and storage costs, which aligns very well with the "high volume low margin" business model.

☆Product Idea #2☆
Ring Size Adjuster

Score: ☆☆☆☆

Similarly to earring backs, ring size adjusters also fall below the product price "sweet spot." However, high sales in this product niche would allow new sellers to enter and operate on high volume.

Moreover, this niche is significantly less competitive than the market for earring backs, which is indicated by only a few hundred search results being returned for "ring size adjuster," and by there being several listings on the front page with a very low number of reviews.

A pro of this product is again that it's very light. The biggest drawback is that this product doesn't allow for a high degree of differentiation. Consider bundling or creating unique packaging to differentiate this product. Finally, high quality photos are a must for this niche.

☆Product Idea #3☆
Crochet Hook Set

Score: ☆☆☆☆☆

This niche allows for a high degree of differentiation, which is indicated by the wide price range for crochet hook sets. Several existing listings fall within the price "sweet spot." Their higher prices are justified by bundling crochet hooks with items such as cases and other crocheting accessories. Most existing listings sell more or less the same types of hooks, made either of rubber or aluminum. Consider how you could differentiate the hooks themselves; e.g., wooden handles. You can also consider designing a stunning case and including your logo on it, and showcasing the case in the product images.

Competition is not too high for this niche, as there are only over 1,000 search results for "crochet hook set," and a majority of listings on the first page have fewer than 100 reviews.

Do research on crocheting in general and read existing reviews in order to identify gaps in the market. You can then use this information to target an underserved niche.

☆Product Idea #4☆
Weaving Ball Winder

Score: ☆☆☆

This is a slightly more complicated product, and might not be best suited for beginners, especially those with a limited amount of money to invest in their first product. For those with a little more money to invest or with more experience, this is an attractive product for 2020.

First, competition is low while estimated sales are quite high. Consider differentiating by having high quality product images, as the photos for existing listings are limited. This does not appear to be a highly brand sensitive niche, as most existing sellers do not have a logo. Consider differentiating by placing your logo on the product itself.

☆Product Idea #5☆
Embroidery Hoops

Score: ☆☆☆☆

While this product may at first glance appear to not allow for much differentiation, in reality there are several ways to differentiate, including ring size, number of pieces, materials used, etc. You can easily differentiate in such a way that the price falls within the "sweet spot."

Determine a way to differentiate your product such that the primary image will stand out. Perhaps you could bundle the embroidery hoops with another item and include both in the primary image. Many of the primary images on the first page look exactly the same, so having a photo that stands out is all the more important.

Competition is low for this niche, with many listings on the first page having few reviews. Consider reading through the lower reviewed listings to identify opportunities for product improvement.

☆Product Idea #6☆
Craft Keeper

Score: ☆☆☆

This isn't a very easy product to differentiate, but if you can manage to get on the first page, you potentially stand to make a lot of sales. Consider your **market focus**: what specific types of customers are you targeting? Most of the craft keepers on Amazon appeal to a wider audience—what specific demographic could you single out and cater to? Children? Young girls? Scrapbookers? Handymen? Modifying your product to directly appeal to certain types of customers can drive sales away from existing sellers who don't have a specific market focus.

The price point for this niche is good. Competition is medium. Consider storage and shipping costs: though the product is light, its dimensions can be rather large, depending on the specific size of your product. This is definitely a riskier product, but as the saying goes: with high risk comes high reward.

☆Product Idea #7☆
Thread Rack

Score: ☆☆☆☆

Thread racks are an attractive product niche as competition is low (only a few hundred search results along with a low average number of reviews) while the price falls well within the $15-40 sweet spot. Many of the listings on the front page are not highly differentiated, but as you scroll down you begin to see more variation; e.g., wall mounted racks, color, materials used, number of spools, etc.

The standard thread rack appears to be wooden and 60-pool. Strongly consider selling a different type of thread rack, as there are several listings for the standard version. Consider putting your logo on the product itself or the packaging as a means of differentiation.

☆Product Idea #8☆
Journal Planner Pens

Score: ☆☆☆

This product niche has a fair level of competition, with over 3,000 search results and a few listings on the first page with greater than 1,000 reviews, but for those able to land on the first page, they potentially stand to make a lot of money. Clearly there is room for entry, as there are several listings on the first page with less than 100 reviews. Many of the listings fall below the price sweet spot, but there are ways to differentiate that would allow for a higher price (such as a higher pen count or bundling).

Many of the listings have more or less the same main image. Consider differentiating your main image in such a way that it would stand out among the many other product listings. Strongly consider bundling so as to justify a higher price. For example, you could include a case for the pens, preferably a visually stunning one, which you can then showcase in your product images.

Books

Score: ☆☆☆☆☆

In 2007 Amazon launched KDP (Kindle Direct Publishing), which has allowed thousands of authors from around the world to easily self-publish their work and receive much more attractive royalties than those of more traditional publishing methods. The main appeal of KDP is that **there is virtually no overhead**, meaning it is possible to publish your work with **zero cost**. You might pay to get your book cover designed, your manuscript to be edited and formatted, or to advertise your book, but these are all optional costs; i.e., you can do all of it yourself.

These next four product ideas will focus on book categories within which anyone could potentially publish, starting with *Small Business and Entrepreneurship*.

As you grow as an entrepreneur, you can begin to share your experiences and what you've learned to aspiring or less experienced entrepreneurs. Here are some topics that are hot right now that almost anyone (with a little bit of research and experience) can write about: Instagram, Facebook, social media marketing in general, motivational topics, passive income, making money online, Amazon, and so on.

☆**Product Idea #10**☆
Spirituality

Score: ★★★☆

For those who are spiritually inclined, this book category can offer an opportunity to express unique views or ways of living a better life. Here are some examples of top selling books in this product category: "The Gifts of Imperfection", "You are a Badass: How to Stop Doubting Your Greatness and Start Living an Awesome Life", and "Daring Greatly: How the Courage to Be Vulnerable Transforms the Way We Live, Love, Parent, and Lead."

If you think you can write something along these lines, then this category is a great fit for you.

☆Product Idea #11☆
Self Help

Score: ★★★★★

There is a lot of overlap between this category and the previous one, and so they are attractive for similar reasons—namely, that there are low barriers to entry to writing a book in these categories. You don't have to be an expert in anything. All you need is to do is pull from personal experience and to be an effective communicator with an idea for a book in these categories.

Here are some topics that are hot right now in self help: effectiveness, negotiation, leadership, habits, and books with aggressive or even profane titles (among the top sellers in this category are "Stop Doing that Sh*t", "The Subtle Art of Not Giving a F*ck", and "Unf*ck Yourself). Clearly books with such titles immediately grab a reader's attention.

☆Product Idea #12☆
Crafts, Hobbies & Home

Score: ☆☆☆☆

Everyone has hobbies, from antiquing to hunting, and gardening to interior design. The list is endless, and depending on your level of skill or experience, you could monetize your knowledge by instructing others on your hobbies.

Here are some more general topics in this category which you might be able to write a book on: dieting, exercise, interior design, organization, cooking, pet care, lifestyle. A lot of these can fall under multiple categories, and when you're publishing your book, Amazon allows you to select up to two categories for your book.

Health and Household

☆Product Idea #13☆
Cigar Case

Score: ☆☆☆☆

One of the best qualities about this product is that it's highly *giftable*. And so a good way to target shoppers who are buying cigar cases as a gift is to include attractive packaging. If you decide to go this route, clearly showcase the packaging (say, a box with your logo on it) in the main image. Shoppers should feel confident enough to directly ship the product to whomever they are gifting it.

There are only over 1,000 search results for "cigar case" and many of the listings on the first page have less 100 reviews; however, listings are generally optimized for this niche, with high quality photos and strong bullet points, indicating that this product niche is competitive. Carefully consider your differentiation strategy with this product: how could you customize it in a way that no existing seller is doing? If you manage to do this and land on the first page, you stand to make some serious cash.

☆Product Idea #14☆
Cigarette Holder

Score: ☆☆☆

What makes this an attractive product is that there are very few sellers; specifically, those targeting women who are buying cigarette holders for a costume. The top sellers don't have very high quality images—there is certainly room here for improvement. Consider having your photographer hire a model to showcase the product with a "Gatsby" or "Roaring 20s" style costume.

Consider bundling in order to raise the price higher than existing listings, otherwise you would be operating by volume (which isn't necessarily a bad thing, given this product is very light and cheap, meaning you can afford to source a much greater quantity).

☆Product Idea #15☆
Tattoo Piercing Bibs

Score: ☆☆☆☆

With this product there is an opportunity to target an *underserved niche*. Most people who want bibs for the purpose of tattooing or piercing end up buying products that advertise themselves as "dental bibs" as well. Sellers are attempting to target customers who are buying for dental purposes and customers who are buying for tattooing/piercing purpose *at the same time*. This potentially creates an opportunity for entry for those who specifically target tattooing and piercing.

The best way you can make it obvious that you are targeting this specific niche is by portraying in the product images how a tattoo artist would use this product. As of the time this book is being written, no existing seller is doing this. Finally, to ensure the long term success of this product, strongly consider creating a brand that aligns with tattooing/piercing.

☆Product Idea #16☆
Purse Organizer Insert

Score: ☆☆☆☆

This product checks all the immediate boxes: less than 1,000 search results, the average price on the front page falls within the sweet spot, and it's a very light product. The average number of reviews on the first page is on the higher side, but average sales are estimated to be high as well.

High quality images and a carefully planned differentiation strategy are a must for this product. Consider your market focus: who exactly are you targeting? What are they using these purse inserts for? Large purses? Handbags? Luxury purses? Ensure that your market focus is not too broad. Catering to a specific niche for this product is likely a precursor to success.

☆Product Idea #17☆
Dust Mask for Kids

Score: ☆☆☆☆

Dust masks have been a hot product on Amazon, but the market has likely gotten too competitive for new entry. There are, however, sub-niches within dust masks that remain attractive, namely, dust masks for kids.

Though there are over 3,000 search results, many of the listings on the front page have very few reviews. Keep in mind that parents are usually willing to pay a premium when it comes to the safety of their kids, which means a higher quality, more expensive product in this market is more likely to do well. Consider a more complicated design that can garner a higher price, and find a supplier that can customize it for use by children.

☆Product Idea #18☆
Bath Tub Pillows

Score: ☆☆☆☆

There are only a few hundred listings for this product, though many of them appear to be quite similar. Differentiation for this product would likely be difficult, but given that there aren't many sellers, this remains an attractive product.

If you read through the customer reviews, you will find that customers often complain that the pillows are too rough, don't wash easily, or don't stay their original color. Clearly there is room for improvement. Consider investing in a higher quality bath pillow and charge a higher price. Fortunately this product is light, and so shipping and storage costs are likely to stay low.

☆Product Idea #19☆
Beard Bib

Score: ☆☆☆☆

Competition is low for this market as the product is relatively new. With only a few hundred current search results and a very low average number of reviews, there is likely room for new entry. Moreover, the price point is good.

High quality product images are a must for this market. Many of the listings on the first page include models using the bibs. Having a strong brand (or the perception of a strong brand) is also recommended; consider including an appealing logo on the product itself. A niche that you can target are people buying this as a gift for someone else—include high quality product packaging and showcase the packaging in the images. Also, you could consider differentiation by design. Most of the existing product are either black or white: how could you design yours so as to make it stand out?

<h2 style="text-align:center">☆Product Idea #20☆</h2>

Tongue Scraper

<h3 style="text-align:center">Score: ☆☆☆</h3>

Though there are several highly optimized listings on the first page, this likely remains an attractive product to sell as there is a relatively small number of existing listings. It's important that your product is 100% BPA free; even if shoppers don't know exactly what this means, they might choose a competitor's product over yours because theirs includes "100% BPA FREE" in the title and yours does not.

Product packaging is important for this market; include high quality packaging and showcase it in your main image. Consider your market focus: are you targeting individuals? Families? People who are travelling? Narrow down your market focus and adjust your product and listing to accommodate your target customer.

Home & Kitchen

☆Product Idea #21☆
Burrito Blanket

Score: ☆☆☆☆

With this particular product it is of utmost importance to clearly define the *market focus*. Again, who are you targeting? Who is your end customer? Babies? Kids? Adults? Couples? Pets? By clearly defining your market focus, you can then modify your product listing accordingly. You *do not* want your main image to be just of the blanket itself. There are many like this already, and your product will not stand out. If you are targeting babies for example, then your main image should be of a baby using the burrito blanket. Also, consider high quality product packaging as a means of differentiation, as this product is very giftable.

This is a hot product right now, and if you can carefully differentiate yourself by focusing on a specific customer group, you stand to potentially make a strong profit.

☆Product Idea #22☆
Step Stool for Kids

Score: ☆☆☆

When it comes to kids' products, it's typically important to consider product safety. Parents and guardians are willing to pay a premium to ensure the safety of their children's products. And with step stools, it's clear that safety is a concern on potential buyers' minds. Having a product specifically geared towards the children's safety is a good way to differentiate your listing in this market.

While there are over 2,000 search results for "step stool for kids," the greater number of existing sellers is justified as this is a high-selling item. If you can manage to get on the first page, you stand to potentially make some serious money. If you are targeting kids for this product, consider how it is being used. Is it meant to be used in the kitchen? Bathroom? The answers to these questions will inform the decisions you'll make regarding the design of the product.

☆Product Idea #23☆
Changing Pad Liners

Score: ★☆☆☆

The average price of this product falls well into the sweet spot. There are less than 1,000 search results; however, most of the listings on the first page are highly optimized, signifying that this is a competitive market. But there are several listings on the front page with a very low number of reviews, so there is likely room for entry. This combined with the fact that this is a well selling item makes it an attractive product for new sellers.

A strong differentiation strategy is critical for success in this market. Most of the existing listings appear to be targeting both girls and boys, so that their product is unisex. Consider designing the product to cater to specifically either boys or girls. If you plan on selling reusable liners, consider marketing the product as "eco-friendly" so as to appeal to parents who are environmentally conscious. In terms of market focus, consider those looking to buy this product as a gift.

☆Product Idea #24☆
Bed Rail for Toddlers

Score: ☆☆☆

There are only over 1,000 search results for this product; however, many of the listings on the first page are highly optimized. But the high number of sales and the higher price point for this product make it an attractive potential product.

Many of the existing listings look more or less the same. There appear to be two types of bed rails, one that more so resembles a rail and another a bumper. Consider how you could design the product so as to make it stand out among the others. For example, a current listing designed the bed numbers to appear like a cat. This a unique idea that makes the product stand out and, moreover, makes it more giftable.

☆Product Idea #25☆
Lollipop Sticks

Score: ☆☆☆

Though this product has a general price that falls below the sweet spot, it remains a potentially lucrative product as it posts high estimated sales and the product is incredibly light, meaning lower shipping and storage costs.

There are over 2,000 search results, though many of the listings on the first page have a very low number of reviews. As always, carefully consider how your product will stand out from the rest. Bundling is an option worth considering for this product as there are likely other items that a potential buyer would be looking for (e.g., wrappers, twist ties) which you can source cheaply.

☆Product Idea #26☆
Sugar Stir Needle

Score: ☆☆☆☆

This product also falls below the sweet spot; what makes it an attractive potential product is the very low competition (less than 200 search results) and high sales volume. Obviously, you don't want to be selling the same 10-piece multicolored set that all the other sellers are selling. Consider sourcing a higher quality stir needle to sell individually. There currently aren't many (if any) sellers doing this right now.

By selling a higher quality needle you can then justify a higher price. To align with a superior product, be sure to have superior product images and to take it a step further, attractive packaging that you can showcase in the product images.

☆Product Idea #27☆
Reusable Coffee Filter

Score: ☆☆☆☆

Reusable products are becoming increasingly popular on Amazon as people in general are growing more environmentally conscious. This creates opportunities for sellers to create entire brands centered around sustainable goods, and reusable coffee filters offer a good entry point for sellers in the more general market of sustainable goods.

There are over 4,000 search results, which is definitely on the higher end of what we're comfortable with, but many of the listings on the front page have a low number of reviews; moreover, there are multiple types of reusable coffee filters, and so depending on your specific product, your market may be narrower. The filters made of hemp cloth seem particularly attractive, as they are incredibly light.

☆Product Idea #28☆
Reusable Silicone Bags

Score: ☆☆☆☆☆

This is another product that takes advantage of the current trend towards more sustainable and environmentally friendly goods. It serves as a substitute for more traditional plastic bags. They are very light, and fall well within the price sweet spot.

There are only over 1,000 search results, and many of the listings on the first page have a low number of reviews. Many of the product images appear more or less the same, so it may be difficult to stand out. If you plan to bundle or include high quality packaging, be sure to showcase it in the main image. Finally, bear in mind that food storage bags come in multiple sizes, and if you plan to offer more than one size this will add complexity to the sourcing process.

☆Product Idea #29☆
5 Gallon Bucket Liner Bags

Score: ☆☆☆☆

This appears to be a good product to sell, at least in the short term, as competition seems to be quite low. There are only a few hundred search results, and many of them are different products entirely. The price point isn't bad, especially considering this would be a cheap and easy product to source.

I say it's likely a good product to sell in the *short term* because this product doesn't allow for much differentiation. Even if it were a good product to sell now, before long other sellers would realize this too and flood the market. If you are considering this a long term product, bear in mind the possibility of increased competition in the future.

☆Product Idea #30☆
Microwave Splatter Cover

Score: ☆☆☆

Though there are less than 1,000 search results for this product, there are a few sellers who appears to dominate the market, each with over 1,000 reviews. Still, there are many sellers on the first page with few reviews and, moreover, this appears to be a high selling item.

If you plan to enter this market, consider not competing directly with one of the bigger sellers. Differentiate your product by catering it to a specific niche that one of the bigger sellers don't directly target. You could sell a higher end splatter cover or introduce some sort of product enhancement, such as a handle to avoid burns.

☆Product Idea #31☆
Fermentation Lids for Mason Jars

Score: ☆☆☆☆☆

This is one of those more obscure products that grab my attention because most sellers would never think to sell something like this. It's an uncommon product (most people probably don't know something like this exists) but there is definitely a market for it. There are less than 500 search results, and the average number of reviews on the first page is very low. Moreover, this would be a cheap product to source.

If you are considering this product, do research on fermentation in general and develop a strong understanding of how customers are using this product. What do they like? What are their complaints? What other items might they need along with the lids? Having a stronger understanding of the customer base will allow you to have a more clearly defined market focus.

☆Product Idea #32☆
Treat Bags with Ties

Score: ☆☆☆

One of the main appeals of this product is that it would be relatively cheap and easy to source. Competition isn't too high, with over 1,000 search results, and the average number of reviews is quite low. The lower price point is fine given that you would be operating by high volume and that the product is cheap to source.

If you plan to sell the standard clear bags with color ties, consider differentiating yourself with superior product images. To avoid competing directly with those selling the same thing, consider designing your product in a unique way while maintaining a general appeal.

☆**Product Idea #33**☆
Strainer Bag for Brewing

Score: ☆☆☆☆☆

This is one of those more niche products that are less commonly known. When you search for "strainer bags for brewing," many of the results appear to call themselves "nut milk bags." It would appear that customers searching for strainer bags for the purpose of brewing are buying these nut milk bags. This suggests that these customers potentially represent an underserved market, which means there's an opportunity.

Consider developing and marketing your strainer bags to cater specifically to those people buying them for the purpose of home brewing. Consider your product packaging. It's easy for this product to go unnoticed if the main image is simply one of the strainer bags themselves; attractive packaging that's showcased in the main image is a good way of catching a shopper's eye.

☆**Product Idea #34**☆
Loose Leaf Tea Infuser

Score: ☆☆☆☆

Here we have another increasingly popular item as a result of the growing trends towards sustainable living. Loose leaf tea infusers allow for a substitute to more traditional tea bags, which create waste. In selling this product, potential sellers should consider various ways they can align the product offering with more environmentally conscious shoppers.

An advanced technique is to donate a certain percentage of all sales to an appropriate charity or fund. If you decide to go this route, be sure to highlight this point in the product listing (at the very least in the product description; consider devoting a product image/infographic to this point).

☆Product Idea #35☆
Silicone Instant Pot Accessories

Score: ☆☆☆☆

There are several silicone instant pot accessories which sell well on Amazon and have relatively low competition. Plus, since they are made of silicone, which is a very light material, shipping and storage costs would be low for such items.

If you are interested in this market you should do research on Instant Pots and all the various ways they can be used. The slings/lifters appear to be a popular item. Keep in mind that it is probably better go after a product with a proven market (assuming you can differentiate) than a completely new product that no one is yet selling, as this exposes you to significant risk.

☆Product Idea #36☆
Wine Glass Markers

Score: ☆☆☆

This item falls below the price sweet spot but makes up for it by being very light and having a strong sales history. Moreover, there are only over 1,000 results for "wine glass markers," and many of the results that come up are different products entirely, signifying that competition within this market isn't too high.

A product listing that isn't highly optimized won't do well in this market. This includes having high quality images, a logo either on the markers themselves, the packaging, or both, and quality packaging that is worth showcasing in the main image.

☆Product Idea #37☆
Jar opener

Score: ☆☆☆☆☆

This is definitely a niche product as it appeals to a very specific audience, namely those with weak or arthritic hands (perhaps there are other niches too). There are many different designs for this product, which allows for greater differentiation. The price point is good, and the product is quite light.

At the risk of sounding like a broken record, I'll say it again: clearly define your market focus. Your market focus will determine the design and listing of your product. Are you targeting your more average customer who is looking for a little help in the kitchen? Or a more senior customer who would really need a heavy duty opener? The answers to these questions will inform much of your product offering, and it's important to know them before you begin sourcing your product.

☆Product Idea #38☆
Sheet straps

Score: ☆☆☆

The main pros of this product are that it's light, sales are estimated to be high, and competition is relatively low (there are only a few hundred search results). The main con, however, is that this is a difficult product to differentiate.

Many of the listings look more or less the same, and many of the existing sellers appear to be competing on price. Therefore, standing out in this market would take a good amount of creativity. Still, the high estimated sales of this product make it worth researching further. Are there any niches within this market that are being underserved? Are there ways to enhance this product which no one has thought of?

☆Product Idea #39☆
Furniture Risers

Score: ☆☆☆☆

The cheaper products in this market likely cater to a niche that is already too crowded. These are the plastic or polypropylene furniture risers that don't look particularly aesthetically pleasing. There is, however, a niche within this market that appears to be less crowded, and it's made up of the higher-end risers made of wood or steel and which have a stylish design.

There aren't many sellers of the higher-end furniture risers an Amazon, likely allowing for ample room for new entry. These are obviously more expensive to source, but since you would be listing them at a higher price, the higher *cost of goods sold* is justified. Your entire product offering should align with the fact that your are selling a higher-end product. This means high quality images and product packaging.

☆**Product Idea #40**☆
Fogless Shaving Mirror

Score: ☆☆☆☆

First, bear in mind that this is a slightly more complicated product to ship, as it is liable to crack or shatter. Competition for this product is relatively low, as there are only a few hundred search results. Most of the existing listings on the first page, however, appear to be highly optimized.

A highly optimized listing is a must in this market, including high quality images (many of the listings include photos with models). Strongly consider reading through all the customer reviews and making a list of potential product enhancements. The average rating for this product is relatively low, and you will likely uncover opportunities by reading through customer complaints.

☆**Product Idea #41**☆
Sagging Couch Support

Score: ☆☆☆☆

This is another great product to sell as competition is relatively low, with just a few hundred search results, while the average price point is well within our sweet spot. The product is on the heavier side and so you should expect to incur greater shipping and storage costs. Another con of this product is that it may be difficult to differentiate.

There definitely appear to be opportunities in this market, however, considering that the average rating of this product is quite low. Many customers complain that the supports don't really make a difference or that they're ineffective. Consider this and other customer complaints you may find in the reviews in determining potential product enhancements.

☆Product Idea #42☆
Couch Clamps for Sectionals

Score: ☆☆☆☆

This product is similar to the previous one in that competition is low while the product itself might be difficult to differentiate. While this product certainly sells at a lower average price, it is much lighter and will incur lower shipping and storage costs.

There are multiple designs for this product, which makes it easier to differentiate. Consider a design which you can market. The simple metal connectors with screws are a harder sell, as this design is very difficult to differentiate. Reach out to various suppliers and see what various designs they can offer; is there one that you can more easily brand or market? Is there a design that would be better suited for attractive product images and/or packaging?

☆Product Idea #43☆
Toy Blocker for Couch

Score: ★★★☆

This is another great product to sell on Amazon as competition appears to be relatively low while the product price falls nicely within our sweet spot. The product itself may be difficult to differentiate, though there are of course other means of differentiation, such as differentiation by brand, by country of origin, by product images, etc. (For a full and detailed list see my guide for beginners.)

The product itself is light, allowing for lower shipping and storage costs. Moreover, the average rating for this product is quite low, which is a great sign for potential sellers. Be sure to read through the customer reviews to uncover ways that you could potentially enhance the product.

☆Product Idea #44☆
Under Door Stopper

Score: ★★★

Compared to the last couple of products, this one has a market that is definitely more competitive. But for good reason: under door stoppers appear to have much greater sales volumes. The price point is good, and it's a relatively light product. There's a good amount of variation in the product design, which is a sign that the product can more easily be differentiated.

The average number of reviews on the first page is quite high, but there are still multiple listings with very few reviews, which means getting on the first page is certainly not impossible. Consider one of the existing designs that does not have so many existing listings. How could you improve on this design? Why are customers buying it and what are they complaining about?

☆Product Idea #45☆
Blackout Film

Score: ★★★

This product makes the list for three reasons: there are variations on this product whose price falls well within our sweet spot, competition is relatively low for the market (with less than 1,000 search results), and the average rating is relatively low, creating opportunities for new entry.

The downsides of this product is that it is comparatively difficult to differentiate the product itself, and there is added complexity as the product typically comes in multiple sizes. Still, there is likely potential for new entry. Be sure to read through the customer reviews, not only for potential enhancements, but to get an understanding of the types of customers that use this product. For example, one review reads, " . . . great for graveyard shift workers." Customer reviews are a great source of information for determining *market focus*.

☆Product Idea #46☆
Glow in the Dark Star Stickers

Score: ★★★

The pros of this product is that it's light and easy to source, the average number of reviews and ratings are relatively low, and there are variations of this product that fall within our price sweet spot.

The product itself does not allow for the highest degree of differentiation. Here we see sellers taking advantage of other means of differentiation, namely, by product origin. In my guide for beginners, I discuss in detail why sourcing from the U.S. can give you a leg up over the competition, as American customers are often willing to pay more for the same product if it's sourced domestically. Be sure to reach out to foreign as well as domestic suppliers and compare costs; does the benefit of sourcing from the U.S justify the higher price?

☆Product Idea #47☆
Oil Burner Pipes

Score: ☆☆☆☆

You can find anything an Amazon, and depending on the type of person you are, this is one of those products you can have fun with and actually enjoy marketing. Competition appears to be very low while the price point falls well within our sweet spot. Keep in made that this product is made of glass, which will add some complexity to the shipping process. Also, if your product breaks on its way to the customer, your product is likely to be returned and you may even receive a negative review.

☆Product Idea #48☆
Log Tote Bag

Score: ☆☆☆☆

This is one of those more niche, less commonly know products that could potentially make for a great item to sell on Amazon. Competition appear to be relatively low, with a few hundred search results; though many of the listings on the first page appear to have high quality main images, which makes for increased competition.

High quality images are a must for this market. Many of the main images appear to be quite similar; consider how you could enhance your product offering in such a way that would allow you to have a main image that stands out. Are people buying this as a gift? If so, you could offer attractive packaging and include it in the main image, which would make your listing stand out from the rest of the pack. Be sure to read through the customer reviews to uncover other potential enhancements.

☆Product Idea #49☆
Fireplace Screen Cover

Score: ☆☆☆☆

As this is a heavier and more expensive product to source, the market has high barriers to entry as many sellers do not have the cash to invest in this product. But for those who do, this is a strong product to consider selling.

Competition is relatively low, with less than 1,000 search results and many of the listings on the first page having very few reviews. Moreover, many of the reviews are rather low. This product will be expensive to source, as they can weigh upwards of fifteen pounds, though sellers are compensated for this by being able to charge upwards of $200 for this product.

☆Product Idea #50☆

Score: ☆☆☆☆

In the more general market of fireplace products and accessories, this product is better suited for beginners or sellers with limited funds. It is more of an obscure product, and so finding a supplier may be more difficult. There is, however, likely room for entry in this market.

Competition is quite low, the average number of reviews are low, and many of the listings aren't optimized, namely in terms of product images. One disadvantage of this product is that it likely does not have a particularly high sales volume, though the market compensates sellers for this by allowing for a high price, and so sellers would be sourcing less units but making a higher profit per unit.

☆Product Idea #51☆
Fireplace Ash Tray

Score: ☆☆☆☆

This fireplace accessory is an attractive product to sell for a lot of the same reasons as the previous product. Competition is relatively quite low and there are a low number of reviews for existing listings. The main difference between this and the previous product is these ash trays are generally heavier, ranging from five to ten pounds. This makes it a more expense product to source and ship per unit; however, the average price of this product is quite high, upwards of $60.

Since there aren't many sellers of this product now, you might be tempted to create a listing with more or less the exact same product as the competitors. This strategy may work in the short term, but in the long term other sellers are bound to enter the market and drive sales away from your listing. Be sure to consider your long-term differentiation strategy so as to prevent losing sales to new sellers.

☆Product Idea #52☆
Ironing Mat

Score: ☆☆☆☆

This is an attractive product to sell as the average number of reviews on the first page appears to be quite low while sales for this product are estimated to be quite high. There is significant overlap between the price range of this product and our price sweet spot. Most of the main images of existing listings appear to be highly optimized; bear this in mind when creating a listing. Consider ways to make your main image stand out; e.g., including high quality packaging or perhaps a pull string bag and showcasing it in the main image.

There are various designs for this product; be sure to differentiate yourself and not sell the standard version of this product. But if you decide to do so, keep in mind you should be differentiating by other means, whether by packaging or product origin or another method.

Industrial and Scientific

☆Product Idea #53☆
Cast Iron Cleaner

Score: ☆☆☆

This market is unique in that while there aren't a great number of sellers, there is one seller with a patented product who dominates the market. Still, there are plenty of competitors' products that sell well. Be sure to not compete directly with the seller who has the patented design by differentiating your product from theirs.

This is a very light product, making it cheap and easy to source and ship. Also, there are multiple variations of it, including a brush and a scrubber meant to be used with a sponge. Consider each design in turn and go with the one for which you expect to have the strongest competitive advantage.

☆Product Idea #54☆
Dryer Vent Cleaner

Score: ☆☆☆

This makes for a good product to sell through Amazon FBA as the product is very light, competition appears to be comparatively low, and there are variations of this product that fall within our price sweet spot. There are a few sellers that source their products from the U.S.; keep this in mind when in the process of sourcing this product.

Dryer vents are one of the leading causes of home fires, and so many customers are buying this product as a preventative measure. Bear this is mind. Try to design your product in such a way that it would be highly effective as a preventative means and be sure to market it as such. Finally, be sure to read through the customer reviews for potential enhancements as there are many reviews for listings on the first page that are quite low.

☆Product Idea #55☆
Urinal Mats

Score: ☆☆☆☆☆

I'm a big fan of products that wouldn't normally be considered "sexy" or a "hot" item. Urinal mats clearly fall in the "unsexy" category, and for this reason alone many sellers are deterred from even considering selling them. This is evident in the relatively low level of competition in this market. Granted, this product does run on the heavier side, which creates a barrier to entry for new sellers as it is more expensive to source. But for those who can afford to source this product they are able to charge a high price, upwards of $50.

If it's not feasible for you to source this item, consider a similar product, Urinal Deodorizers. These are much lighter and easier to source, while remaining an attractive product for potential sellers.

☆Product Idea #56☆
Kleenex Wall Holder

Score: ☆☆☆☆☆

This again is one of those more obscure products, and it's one that checks all the immediate boxes. It's light, competition appears to be relatively low, the price is right, and the average rating on the first page is not too high, creating opportunities for new entrants to improve the product.

Read through the customer reviews not only for potential enhancements, but also to get a better idea of your customers. Segment them into groups and determine your market focus; in other words, the types of customers you plan on targeting.

☆Product Idea #57☆
Napkin Receptacle

Score: ☆☆☆☆

Many experienced Amazon sellers will prescribe only selling products that weigh less than two pounds. But this is an outdated way of thinking. As competition increases on Amazon, sellers need to look for opportunities in areas where they haven't in the past. This product falls outside this prescribed range (though not by too much); still, it remains an attractive product as competition appears to be relatively low and the price point itself is attractive as well.

Be sure to segment the customers for this product. Again, what is your market focus? Offices? Individuals? Office workers? Individual buying for their household? Again, having a clearly defined market focus is a prerequisite to how you create your listing and how you decide to differentiate your product.

☆Product Idea #58☆
Dolly Moving Straps

Score: ☆☆☆☆

This product is attractive for prospective sellers for multiple reasons: the price is high relative to the weight of the product, competition isn't too high, with about 500 search results, and there are several listings on the first page with a low number of reviews.

The main downside to this product, however, is that it may be difficult to differentiate. Again, be sure to read through customer reviews for potential enhancements. For example, many complain of one of the top selling listings that the straps are too short, not allowing for the carrying of larger items. Just with this piece of information alone you can image who you might differentiate and market your product as one that is suitable for ALL types of furniture, no matter the size.

☆Product Idea #59☆
Construction Protractor

Score: ☆☆☆

This makes for a good product to sell for multiple reasons. The product is very light, for the right kind of design you can charge a high price within our sweet spot, and competition seems to be comparatively low.

One thing to consider and do further research on is brand sensitivity in this market. How likely are customers to default to buying products whose brands they recognize in this market? Many of the existing protractors appear to have a logo or at least the company name on them, so there might be some degree of brand loyalty in this market.

☆Product Idea #60☆
Ring Toss Game

Score: ☆☆☆☆

There are many types of ring toss games, but the one that caught my eye as a potential opportunity is the hook and ring toss game that you might find at certain bars, especially bars with games or outdoor bars. There aren't too many selling this product right now, and they are able to charge a pretty high price.

Consider your customers. Who's buying this product? Individual for their household? Bar owners or managers? Something that I would look into is the quantity of this product that customers typically buy. I've often seen two, three, or even more of these in a given bar, and so there may be an opportunity to sell this item in packs.

☆Product Idea #61☆
Hanger Stacker

Score: ☆☆☆☆

To be honest, I didn't even know this product existed until I uncovered it in my product research. And this for me is a good sign, as this may be one of those more obscure products that isn't on most sellers' radars. There are only about 500 search results, and the average number of ratings is quite low, which likely makes getting on the first page less difficult.

The primary disadvantage of this product is that it's likely hard to differentiate. Many of the existing listings appear to be more or less the same (though there appear to be two variations on the design) and the product itself isn't too complicated. There are, however, a few listings that offer a very different design; e.g., a much taller stacker. Consider improving on such designs if you plan to enter this market.

Kitchen & Dining

★Product Idea #62★
Deviled Egg Tray

Score: ★★★

There appears to be relatively little competition in this market. Furthermore, there are more specific niches or submarkets within this market, such as serving trays and storage trays. Be sure to analyze each of these submarkets separately, and ask yourself: do you plan to sell serving or storage trays? Is it possible to design a tray that would suffice for both purposes?

There is naturally much more variation in the serving tray niche, given the infinite number of ways you could design them to be aesthetically pleasing. Bear in mind that it may be difficult to come up with a design that would have a more general appeal. There isn't as much variation for those trays that you can use to store deviled eggs. Consider a design that could be used for both storing and serving. Finally, keep in mind that this product may experience some seasonality.

★Product Idea #63★
Bread Basket with Warming Stone

Score: ★★★★

Here we have another product I had no idea existed (perhaps due merely to my own ignorance). Anyway, the competition for this product is quite low; there aren't many sellers offering this product. Moreover, the product is not too heavy, allowing for low shipping and storage costs.

The top seller of this product (at the time this book is being written) doesn't have highly optimize product images, which is a sign that there is room for entry in this market. Read through existing customer reviews; they aren't particularly high for this product. Find potential product enhancements and incorporate them into your own product.

☆Product Idea #64☆
Cupcake Stand LED

Score: ☆☆☆

This is certainly a niche product, and so naturally sales aren't going to be as high as, say, some product you could find in every household. Still, there aren't many sellers offering this product, and there are plenty on the first page with a low number of reviews. The product can run more than two pounds, though the average price is well within our sweet spot of $15-40.

In looking through the first page it appears there isn't much to distinguish most of the listings, and so it may be difficult to differentiate this product. However you differentiate, be sure to reflect this in your main image in such a way that it stands out from the other sellers' images.

☆Product Idea #65☆
Cutter Bowl

Score: ☆☆☆

The first page for this product contains many listings that appear more or less the same. This does not favor a strong differentiation strategy; however, given that there are not too many sellers offering this product and sales are estimated to be high, this is a potential product worth considering.

The ratings for existings listings aren't particularly high, and in the reviews there are countless ways which customers have given to improve the product; for example, having a cutter bowl that allows cutting at multiple angles. Read through the reviews and make a list of potential product enhancements, and then reach out to various suppliers to see whether they can manufacture the product accordingly.

☆Product Idea #66☆
Napkin Rings Set

Score: ☆☆☆

This is a product that allows for a wide range of creativity in terms of design. There are countless designs, from more standard wooden rings to ones that are holiday themed. There are over 2,000 results for this search term, but if you can manage to get on the first page, you potentially stand to make some serious profit.

Be sure that your design isn't *too* niche. Something like a flamingo design is too specific to appeal to enough customers. Think about who you're selling to. Households? Restaurants? Maybe there are certain types of restaurants that are currently being underserved. And if you are targeting restaurants, carefully consider your quantity per order; it wouldn't make sense to sell these individually.

Office Products

☆Product Idea #67☆
Self Adhesive Cork Tiles

Score: ☆☆☆

These self adhesive cork tiles make for an attractive product to sell for two main reasons: competition is quite low while estimated sales are high. There aren't too many search results for this product, and on the first page there are multiple listings with less than 100 reviews. The main con of this product (like a good number of other products) is that it does not clearly allow for much differentiation.

To uncover forms of differentiation we must dive into the customer reviews and learn how customers are using this product. Some people use this to hang items such as jewelry. How much weight can these tiles support? Perhaps it would be profitable to design a product that can support more weight so as to cater to this underserved niche. Ask yourself: what customers are constantly complaining and how can I serve them better than existing sellers?

☆Product Idea #68☆
Book Rack for Classroom

Score: ☆☆☆

Here we have a product that allows for a great degree of differentiation, as evident in the search results where no two items appear to be exactly the same. In general, the price of this product falls well within our sweet spot, some far exceeding it, though these are much heavier items that wouldn't be practical for beginners.

Still, some of the lower priced racks exceed the prescribed two pounds by a fair amount, and so new sellers should keep this in mind if considering selling this product. This may be more suitable as a second or third product to sell on Amazon, though it's possible to create a cheaper and simpler variation which might sell well.

☆Product Idea #69☆
Locker Kit

Score: ☆☆☆☆

This is another product that likely allows for ample variation for new entry. Many of the listings on the front page fall within the price sweet spot. When selling this product one should consider if they are targeting male or female students, or whether they plan to go for a unisex design. A unisex design may appeal to a wider audience, though you may lose sales to those sellers who are specifically targeting either boys or girls.

Keep in mind that this product experiences seasonality, as sales spike at the end of summer when schools resume. This may be a product not suitable to be sourced year round but rather once a year.

☆Product Idea #70☆
Floor Cushions for Classroom

Score: ☆☆☆☆

As this product is meant for an entire classroom, they are generally sold in packs of four or six, which causes the price and the weight of the product per unit to be on the higher end. Still, there are many indications that the market has room for entry.

First, the product allows for ample differentiation. Second, the top sellers of this product don't have very many reviews. Landing a spot on the first page wouldn't be as difficult as for a market whose top seller has, say, thousands of reviews.

☆Product Idea #71☆
Business Card Holder for Desk for Women

Score: ☆☆☆☆☆

This product idea showcases the benefits of determining a *market focus*. Searching for "business card holder for desk" yields over 5,000 results on Amazon. You'll find that a majority of these are either geared towards men or are unisex. The same search appended with "for women" gives us just over 1,000 results. By considering potential customer groups who are currently underserved in a given market, we can uncover potential opportunities. Here, it is likely that the "business card holder for desk" market is too competitive, though the niche geared towards women is more likely to have room for new entry.

☆Product Idea #72☆
Pocket Charts for Classroom

Score: ☆☆☆☆

Here we have a generally light product whose market has a high degree of variation. Since the product is so light, consider selling them in packs so that your per unit price falls within the sweet spot. Be sure to research the many types of pocket charts, and go after one that isn't too niche. This is already such a unique product that entering a niche within this market that is too specific would likely lead to insufficient sales.

The average number of reviews on the first page is quite low, which is obviously a good sign for potential new sellers. Be sure to read through the customer reviews to identify potential enhancements for this product.

☆Product Idea #73☆
Braille Writing Slate

Score: ☆☆☆

This is a relatively small market, and so sales are likely to be lower than some of the other products on this list. But that doesn't mean you can't have a big *profit*. This is a very light product, and so shipping and storage costs would be quite low. Most of the existing listings don't appear to be highly optimized, and most of them also appear to be more or less the same product. In order to make a higher profit, consider offering one of the larger slates that fall within the price sweet spot.

Ask yourself, who's buying these products? Perhaps teachers for a classroom? If that's the case, then there's an opportunity to sell this product in larger packs as no seller is currently doing this.

☆Product Idea #74☆
Chair Bands

Score: ☆☆☆

Here we have a high-selling item, as indicated by the number of search results and the degree to which many of the existing listings are optimized. Perhaps a year ago I would've given this product a score of four or even five stars, but clearly since then the market has gotten increasingly competitive.

Still, there may be some room for new entry, as the average number of reviews on the first page isn't too high and there are plenty of listings that are reviewed poorly. As you consider a strategy to differentiate this product, think about how you could make the main image stand out among the many other sellers.

Patio, Lawn & Garden

☆Product Idea #75☆
Leaf Bag Holder Stand

Score: ☆☆☆☆☆

This is one of those products that for me just about checks every box. The one possible con of this product is that it generally runs on the heavier side; but as I've stated previously in this book, it is becoming increasingly profitable to go after markets that Amazon sellers have traditionally avoided; e.g., heavier products that incur greater shipping and storage costs. You are rewarded in this market for higher costs with a higher price, upwards of $30.

Another advantage of this product is that there are many types of leaf bag holder stands. Consider the various designs, how they sell, and how they can be improved or enhanced.

☆Product Idea #76☆
Yard Waste Tarp

Score: ☆☆☆☆

This is another great product in Patio, Lawn & Garden, as competition appears to be quite low, with less than a couple hundred reviews and many of the top sellers having photos that aren't optimized, and the price falls nicely within our sweet spot. Moreover, the product is not too heavy.

Read through existing reviews for potential enhancements. An important feature of this product are its handles—how could you enhance the handles or how a customer might haul the tarp? Finally, bear in mind that this product likely experiences seasonality, as yard work that would require such a product is more common in the Fall.

☆Product Idea #77☆
Knee Pads for Gardening

Score: ☆☆☆

Though competition specifically within the "knee pads for gardening" market may not appear to be too high, one must consider the various _substitutes_ for this product. In my guide for beginners, I go over how to measure the _threat of substitutes_ in assessing the overall competitiveness of a market. It is a key aspect of competition, and you should always ask yourself what the substitute products are for your specific product. For this particular product, there are kneeling pads, stools, rolling seats, etc. All of a sudden, after considering substitute products, we see that this market is much more competitive than we first thought.

Still, there appear to be some opportunities in the submarket of knee pads. For starters, there don't appear to be many listings with product designs that are clearly geared towards women. Furthermore, many customers complain that some of the existing products aren't meant for more heavy garden work. Be sure to read through the many customer reviews for potential enhancement opportunities.

☆Product Idea #78☆
Greenhouse Hoops

Score: ☆☆☆☆☆

As far as obscure products go, this one is up there. Only a few hundred search results, low average number of reviews, a good price point, variations that weigh less than two pounds—this product checks all the immediate boxes.

If you are considering selling this product, do your research. Chances are you (like me) know nothing about greenhouses. Learn what you need to, and anticipate potential customer complaints before they arise.

☆Product Idea #79☆
Outdoor Fountain Cover

Score: ☆☆☆

What makes this a challenging market is that this is not a "one size fits all" sort of product. Fountains obviously come in various sizes, and so you would either have to offer multiple sizes or pick a specific size to sell. Still, what's attractive about this market is that for a higher quality cover, you can charge a premium, as evident by some of the listings being priced over $100.

Again, do your research. What are the most common sizes of outdoor fountains? Why are some of the existing covers reviewed so poorly? What sort of material is ideal for covers? Keep in mind that putting in the work to research a more obscure product can potentially be well worth the effort—it's this effort that often creates a barrier to entry for less motivated sellers.

☆**Product Idea #80**☆
Mailbox Flag Replacement

Score: ☆☆☆

This is one of those products that would be very easy to source, and it may be worth it given that competition doesn't appear to be too high (based on there being only a few hundred search results) and that the price point isn't bad.

The problem with this product is that you can't expect significant long term profits. If this is an opportunity that simply isn't on many sellers' radars, eventually it will be, and existing sellers who are enjoying a high profit margin might find themselves in a situation where they are forced to compete on price. That being said, you probably shouldn't depend on this product in the long term.

☆**Product Idea #81**☆
Rain Chain Gutter Adapter

Score: ☆☆☆

This may very well be the most obscure product on this list. There aren't too many sellers in this market and the average number of reviews on the first page is quite low; however, you should consider whether this market is too small for new entry.

Most of the existing adapters appear to be unique to particular rain chains. Obviously, a new seller would look to design and sell an adapter that can be used for all rain chains. It appears that those few sellers who are doing this are able to charge a high price for something that is very light and likely cheap to source.

☆Product Idea #82☆
Hammock Chair

Score: ☆☆☆

Though there are less than 1,000 search results for this product, it's clear by how optimized the existing product listings are that this is a competitive market. Moreover, this is a heavier and more expensive product, and so it's likely not suitable for less experienced sellers or those with limited funds.

For those who are interested in this product, if you can manage to secure a spot on the first page, you stand to potentially make some serious profit. This is clearly a more luxury item that people are willing to pay a high price for. The reviews for existing products aren't particularly high, so be sure to comb them for potential enhancements.

☆Product Idea #83☆
Fruit Fly Paper

Score: ☆☆☆☆

This is one of those products that clearly aren't "sexy," which is a good things for sellers who know better than to go after those sexier or hotter ticket items that everyone else is trying to sell. In looking through just the first page for this product, you already see all the various substitutes for this product; in fact there are just as many (if not more) products on the first page that *aren't* fruit fly paper.

Still, this is a light product that would be cheap to source. Even though the price of the product falls a bit below our sweet spot, this is permissible given that the product is so light. Be sure, as always, to determine a plan for differentiation. A brilliant example of this is a seller who designed their paper in the shape of butterflies so as to make it more aesthetically pleasing around a house.

☆Product Idea #84☆
Big Rat Traps

Score: ☆☆☆☆

While "rat traps" in general are likely too broad of a market to compete in, the "big rat traps" market is more attractively sized for new entry. There is a good amount of variation on product design, some of which are smaller and cheaper and more suitable for new sellers or those with a limited budget.

Several of the listings on the first page don't have the highest reviews, so be sure to read through them for potential enhancements. Again, there are multiple designs for this product, from heavy duty and electric traps to humane ones. Be sure to read reviews for each and assess where there is the greatest room for improvement.

☆Product Idea #85☆
Pool Cover Water Tubes

Score: ☆☆☆☆

There is clearly room for new entry in this market. Ratings are pretty low (despite being numerous, meaning there are a lot of complaints) and listings aren't highly optimized. The biggest barrier to entry is that these tubes are sold in packs, leading to a high weight per unit, which means higher storage costs. Still, you are able to charge a high price, which offsets the higher cost.

Carefully consider how you plan to differentiate this product. Most of the listings appear to be more or less the same; consider how you may have a main image that would stand out from the rest.

☆Product Idea #86☆
Saluspa Drink Holder

Score: ☆☆☆☆

Here we have a very niche product that most likely is not on a given seller's radar. One sign that this market is not too competitive is that there are no "sponsored" products that come up when you search for "saluspa drink holder." Amazon sellers pay for their products to come up as "sponsored" through an advertising program called Pay Per Click (PPC). For more about PPC, see my guide.

The average price of this product falls nicely within our sweet spot. One concern to bear in mind is that, given this is such a niche product, you may find difficulty in finding a supplier. *Supplier power* is a key component in assessing the competitiveness of a niche. The less suppliers there are, the less power you have as a business to demand a lower price by having suppliers compete for your business.

Sports & Outdoors

☆Product Idea #87☆
Traction Cleats

Score: ☆☆☆

This is definitely a hot item on Amazon, and a year ago I would have given it a score of four or five stars. Now, however, competition has increased as a multitude of sellers have entered the market. Still, it's worth considering this market as sales are estimated to be quite high.

The strongest indication that there is some room for new entry is given by the fact that there numerous listings on the first page with a low number of reviews. Many of them are rated four stars or above, though there are some with less than four stars. If you do plan to enter this market, success will likely hinge on your ability to carve out a very specific niche within the market.

☆Product Idea #88☆
Shoulder Holster

Score: ☆☆☆☆

Some people may be opposed to selling such an item due to personal views. From the perspective of business, you can think of this as a kind of barrier to entry, in that not all sellers would be willing to sell this product.

While there are over 3,000 search results, which is on the high side, you will find that there are multiple designs for this product, which creates niches within the market and greater opportunities for differentiation. Be sure to read through the customer reviews to get a sense of all the types of customers that buy this product. From there you can define your market focus, which would ideally be an underserved customer group or a niche whose product could be significantly improved.

☆Product Idea #89☆
Personal Pocket Bag Left Shoulder

Score: ☆☆☆

While there are less than 500 search results for this product, the market appears to be competitive, as many of the listings on the first page are highly optimized. Therefore, success in this market is likely dependent on a seller's ability to carve out a specific niche to target.

There is likely room for entry, as many of the listings on the first page have a low number of reviews and are rated four star or below. Again, anytime this is the case, you should read through as many customer reviews as you can for insights on how to improve the product. Consider underserved customers; for example, most of the existing products appear to appeal to men or are unisex—how big is the market of this product for women?

☆Product Idea #90☆
Silicone Sleeve

Score: ☆☆☆☆

Don't be overwhelmed by the over 20,000 search results for the keyword "silicone sleeve." There are numerous submarkets within this more general market; e.g., silicone sleeves for for mason jars, wine glasses, water bottles, etc. Be sure to search for each of these in turn, and assess the attractiveness of each market.

If you begin to type "silicone sleeves for," Amazon will give you a list of suggested searches. You could surmise that the first suggestions are the most popular (though who knows how Amazon's algorithms work). For example, when I do this the first suggested result is "silicone sleeves for roller bottles."

In general, this is a light product that would be very cheap and easy to ship. Try to find a niche that would allow for greater differentiation, especially one that allows for higher prices. Keep in mind potential substitutes, as silicone is not the only material that can be used to make such sleeves.

☆**Product Idea #91**☆
Cedar Closet Moth Protection

Score: ☆☆☆☆☆

Here we have another obscure product, and I'm basing this in part on the fact that I didn't know such a thing existed. Cedar is apparently a natural pesticide, and when used in your closet prevents pests such as silverfish from coming in contact with your clothes. Admittedly during my research I actually bought this product for myself, as I've had to deal with silverfish in my clothes several times in the past.

The weight of this product is not too high (depending on the specific design), the price is right, and competition does not seem to be too high. Be sure to perform the necessary due diligence and plan a differentiation strategy. There are already highly optimized listings in this market, and there are likely to be more in the future. A listing that does well today will not maintain the same sales tomorrow unless they prepare in advance to compete with new sellers entering the market.

☆Product Idea #92☆
Unisex Potty Urinal

Score: ☆☆☆☆

This is another one of those product I like for the sole reason that it's not "sexy." While the market for this product is not huge, there is likely room for entry. Consider your market focus and how each type of customer uses this product. Is this something that people would ever share? Or are they most likely to use it individually? Who are you targeting? Men? Women? Boys? Girls? Given the nature of the product, there is a market for each of these customer groups.

Consider each market in turn and assess which you should enter first. You may in the future create a brand under which you have multiple types of potty urinals geared towards both sexes and various ages.

☆Product Idea #93☆
Medal Holder for Kids

Score: ☆☆☆☆

This product offers an attractive ratio of price to weight. The product itself is not too heavy while the price generally ranges from $20 to $50; it's not too common to find such a high price for this light of a product. Furthermore, there doesn't appear to be that many sellers currently offering this product, though it does not readily seem to be easy to differentiate.

Consider the various niches. You could target based on gender, sport, or you could have some sort of inspirational slogan on the product, such as "Never give up." These are only the ways existing sellers are differentiating their products, and you may think of a unique way to differentiate that no existing sellers has.

☆Product Idea #94☆
Boat Cover Support Pole

Score: ☆☆☆☆

Another obscure product, and one that checks a lot of boxes: good price point, light, low average number of reviews on the first page, and several listings rated below four stars.

If you're like me and don't know anything about boating, be sure to do your due diligence and learn about boating in general and specifically how this product is used. As always, a great place to begin is the customer reviews. For this particular product, there is a bountiful source of customer complaints, which is great for a potential seller.

☆Product Idea #95☆
Motor Hood Cover

Score: ☆☆☆☆

Here we have another boating product that is perhaps a little less obscure than the previous one but that still checks a lot of our immediate boxes: an attractive price range for sellers, opportunities for product enhancement or improvement as indicated by low customers reviews, and a market that overall does not appear to be over competitive.

As with the previous product, do your due diligence. Familiarize yourself with boating in general and how this product is being used. The worst case scenario that would result from inadequate due diligence is discovering a significant oversight on your part in the product design that would lead to bad reviews and ultimately no sales.

☆Product Idea #96☆
Spikeball Replacement Balls

Score: ☆☆☆☆

Spikeball is a relatively new phenomenon in the area of leisurely sports, which makes for new opportunities for potential sellers. Begin typing "spike ball" into Amazon and you'll probably see that among the first several suggested searches are "spike ball balls" and "spike ball ball replacement." Clearly there is demand.

In reading the customer reviews for the original Spikeball replacement balls, it seems customers are complaining that the glow in the dark balls don't actually glow very much. People want to play in the dark or dim light, so this is a specific niche that you can target. Perhaps you can bundle a superior glow in the dark ball with something that can be fixed to the rim of the net so that it glows as well. This is just one way you could potentially differentiate yourself, and there are likely others that you should explore.

☆Product Idea #97☆
Dazzler Ribbons

Score: ☆☆☆

You can immediately tell that this market likely has a low level of competition by the fact that there are no sponsored products. So a question you have to ask yourself is: is this market too small? And also, how static is the market? Can I grow the market by introducing a product that targets an underserved niche?

The answers to these questions are likely to be found in the customer reviews. Not many sellers are offering this product, and among those that do many of them have low reviews. Start here. Are there customer complaints that no existing seller is addressing with their product? If so, then you may have an opportunity to not only enter but expand the market.

Tools & Home Improvement

☆Product Idea #98☆
Magnetic Wristband

Score: ☆☆☆☆

This product makes for a great stocking stuffer and, more generally, a great gift. The price point is good relative to the weight of the product, there aren't that many sellers offering this product, and there are multiple listings on the first page with a low number of reviews.

However, even though there are relatively few sellers in this market, it regardless appears to be competitive as many of the listings are highly optimized. Scanning the first page, you see that many of the listings appear at first glance more or less the same. Therefore you must think hard about how you could make your main image stand out. Keep in mind that this product is highly giftable, making packaging an important factor. Consider providing high quality packaging that you could showcase in the main image.

☆Product Idea #99☆
Hat Rack for Closet

Score: ☆☆☆

This is another one of those product that is well suited for Amazon FBA, and plenty of sellers have taken notice. In other words, the market is competitive. This is indicated by there being over 3,000 search results, there being multiple substitutes for any given design of this product, and there being listings on the first page with reviews in the thousands.

Still, this appears to be a high selling item, and so the market is worth analyzing further. To perhaps beat a dead horse: customer reviews are the best place to start. How can you improve one of the existing designs? How can you differentiate your product in such a way that would ensure a long term competitive advantage?

☆Product Idea #100☆
Drain Clog Remover

Score: ☆☆☆

This is another one of those "unsexy" products that you should train your eye to catch. See what others don't, and you will have a leg up over the competition. Anyway, to get back to the product, you'll notice that the price generally falls below our sweet spot. This is okay, given that this would be such a cheap and easy product to source.

How do you plan to differentiate this product? There are already multiple sellers bundling the product with other drain cleaning accessories. Is there an alternative bundling scheme that you can think of? If not, how else could you differentiate this product? By product origin? By packaging? If you are not able to determine a sufficient plan for differentiation for this product, than you should proceed to find others.

☆Product Idea #101☆
Shower Door Bottom Seal

Score: ★★★

We've come to the last product on our list.

Here we have a product not offered by too many existing sellers, at a good price point, with plenty of listings with a low number of reviews, that is light, but one that does not allow for much differentiation.

But this is likely a high selling item, which makes it worth considering. Get creative with your main image. How can you make it stand out from the rest? Read through the customer reviews. Is there an underserved niche within this market? The answers to these questions will inform your decision to source this product and how you structure the product offering.

Phew! We're finally at the end.

Over the course of this book we've gone over 101 products that you could potentially source from Amazon. To perhaps state the obvious, bear in mind that you are not the only one reading this book. And so it's likely that there will be other sellers going after the products on this list. My hope is that, beyond merely a list of product ideas, this book has demonstrated to you the logic and thought that experienced sellers undergo when selecting products.

Of course, the purpose of this book is not to expound a systematic way of performing product research and selecting products to sell on Amazon. For that, I highly recommend you take a look at my guide for beginners, *7 FBA Secrets that Turn Beginners into Best Sellers*.

Additionally, I will soon release the **Official Video Series** to accompany the guide, which will provide you hours of more in-depth instruction on how to make an income on Amazon. Be sure to sign up using the link below and you will be notified as soon as the videos are made available. Plus, I'll send you the actual spreadsheet (a companion to the guide) that I use to conduct my product research and competitive analysis.

Looking forward to continuing this journey with you!

—Matt

Links

Amazon FBA Master Spreadsheet:
https://mailchi.mp/076331bf184b/getthefreefbaspreadsheet

How to Sell on Amazon in 2020: 7 FBA Secrets that Turn Beginners into Best Sellers:
https://www.amazon.com/dp/1705644651

Made in the USA
Las Vegas, NV
19 November 2020